OPTIONS TRADING CRASH COURSE

THE ULTIMATE AND COMPLETE GUIDE FOR BEGINNERS TO START TRADING IN OPTIONS WITH THE BEST AND PROFITABLE STRATEGIES TO QUIT YOUR JOB AND MAKE A LONG-TERM PASSIVE INCOME.

BY
DONALD E. SIMONS

© **Copyright 2021 - All rights reserved.**

The content contained within this book may not be reproduced, duplicated or transmitted without direct written permission from the author or the publisher.

Under no circumstances will any blame or legal responsibility be held against the publisher, or author, for any damages, reparation, or monetary loss due to the information contained within this book. Either directly or indirectly.

Legal Notice:

This book is copyright protected. This book is only for personal use. You cannot amend, distribute, sell, use, quote or paraphrase any part, or the content within this book, without the consent of the author or publisher.

Disclaimer Notice:

Please note the information contained within this document is for educational and entertainment purposes only. All effort has been executed to present accurate, up to date, and reliable, complete information. No warranties of any kind are declared or implied. Readers acknowledge that the author is not engaging in the rendering of legal, financial, medical or professional advice. The content within this book has been derived from various sources. Please consult a licensed professional before attempting any techniques outlined in this book.

By reading this document, the reader agrees that under no circumstances is the author responsible for any losses, direct or indirect, which are incurred as a result of the use of information contained within this document, including, but not limited to, — errors, omissions, or inaccuracies.

Table of Contents

INTRODUCTION 4

CHAPTER 1. MINDSET FOR TRADER 8

CHAPTER 2. WHAT AN OPTION IS AND TYPES 13

CHAPTER 3. HOW TO GET STARTED IN OPTIONS TRADING 19

CHAPTER 4. OPTIONS STRATEGIES 26

CHAPTER 5. HOW TO MAXIMIZE PROFITS 31

CHAPTER 6. RISK MANAGEMENT 37

CHAPTER 7. TIPS AND TRICKS 43

CHAPTER 8. PRACTICAL EXAMPLES AND STRATEGIES 49

CHAPTER 9. POINTS OF INTEREST FOR OPTIONS TRADING 58

CHAPTER 10. RULES FOR SUCCESSFUL TRADING 64

CHAPTER 11. MISTAKES TO AVOID IN OPTIONS TRADING . 70

CHAPTER 12. WHEN TO ENTER AND EXIT THE TRADE 75

CONCLUSION 80

Introduction

Options trading is a high-risk, high-reward market. However, it can be a great way to make some money if you're willing to learn.

Options are a type of derivative. This means that they can be bought or sold on futures markets. They are also called "options contracts." When anyone buys an option contract, they agree at a certain point in the future to buy or sell a quality at a certain amount. The buyer does not get the asset; they just agree to exchange it for money when the contract expires.

Options trading is also referred to as "call" and "put" trading, which refers to whether the options are buying or selling an asset in the future. Buying calls means you hope the price of something goes up. Selling calls means you hope that the price of something goes down. Buying puts means you hope the price of something goes down more than it will go up. Selling puts means you hope that the price of something goes up more than it will go down. You can see how options trading is similar to gambling in some ways!

No matter which type of option we are talking about, both of them have a predetermined price at which you have to either sell the option or buy it, and this particular price is termed as the strike price.

In order to complete the groundwork, you should understand each term, and so, here are several key terms that are used very frequently in options trading.

Intrinsic Value: If I have to explain in very simple words, then I would say that an asset's value is determined by its intrinsic value. There is a complex financial model and an objective calculation that are implemented in order to find the intrinsic value of an option. There are several meanings to intrinsic value, and it is based on the area of application. So, this is just an umbrella term. The strike price, when subtracted from the price of the underlying security of the option when it is in the money, gives the measure of the intrinsic value. Here is an example to make it even clearer. Suppose the strike price of a call option is $25, and the stock underlying that option is being traded at $27, then the intrinsic value of that particular option is $2.

Extrinsic Value: The difference between the intrinsic value and the premium of a particular option gives the extrinsic value. In the above example, if the price at which the actual option is being traded is $2.50, then the extrinsic value is $0.50. There is another term that is used to denote the extrinsic value of an option; that is, time value.

In-the-Money: When an option has an intrinsic value is when the term in-the-money or ITM is used. In simpler terms, if you compare with the underlying asset's market price, then the value in the strike price is in your favor. These two points should make it even clearer:

- When the holder of the option has a scope of buying the underlying security at a value that is lesser than the present market price, then that is referred to as in 'in-the-money call option.'
- When the holder of the option has a scope of selling the underlying security at a value that is more than the present market price, then that is referred to as an 'in-the-money put option.'

You should also be aware of the idea of parity whenever you are talking about in-the-option. There is parity in the option if the intrinsic value is equal to the option price. Similarly, the option will be trading at a level above parity when the price of the option is greater than the intrinsic value.

When the option price is less than the intrinsic value, then the option will be trading at a level below parity. Usually, the options trade at a level above parity. Let us assume that the trading price of each share of an XYZ company is $100; then it will be trading above parity when the May 95 call is greater than $5 (the price of the option is more than the intrinsic value). It will be trading at parity when the May 95 call is at $5 (the intrinsic value is equal to the option price), and similarly, it will be trading below parity if the May 95 call is less than $5 (option price is less than the intrinsic value).

At-the-Money: When the present trading price of an underlying asset is close to or the same as the option's strike price, then it is called at-the-money or ATM. For example, if the trading price of each share of an XYZ company is $100, then the January 100 put and January 100 call are at-the-money. Even if the per-share price is $99, then too the January 100 put and January 100 call is said to be at-the-money. But sometimes, the term 'near-the-money' is used to describe such a phenomenon. There is no inherent value associated with the ATM option, but before the expiration date, they may have a time value. In simpler words, when exercised, the ATM options are not in any position to fetch you a profit from the trade. But if the expiration date has not approached, then they still possess value. If you are guessing that there will be a huge stock movement, then the ATM options are going to be very attractive.

There are many advantages to trading options, but there are also disadvantages. Traders who aren't familiar with all of the various trading options will make uninformed risks that can potentially lead to loss of money or be detrimental to their desired financial goals.

It is important for traders to be familiar with the various options available, both in terms of their basic characteristics and the types of risks each poses.

When used wisely, options can provide much-needed flexibility for a trader that can help them achieve their goals.

Options trading gives you more control over your trading than other forms of investment do. You avoid some risk by limiting your losses but still have some possibility for gains. Options give you some leverage on the market because your purchase price can be lower than the current market price—you could theoretically profit if the price of an underlying asset moves substantially upward.

Chapter 1. Mindset for Trader

A successful options trader is a unique individual. This person learns how to leverage their financial position to pave a way to profitable returns that make the time and effort invested worth it. This person is strong-willed and determined.

The truth is even though everyone can understand these concepts and maybe the ability to implement these strategies, not everyone has the fortitude to stick with it until they gain the results they want—which is financial freedom. The people that do, fall into a small bracket. A strong options trader requires a unique set of skills, attitude, and personality.

The Traits of a Successful Options Trader

- **Being self-disciplined.** You may be excited about the possibility of gaining financial freedom by using options trading. If you are willing to jump with both feet in, I applaud you. I also implore you to exercise caution and, therefore, self-discipline. Do not just stop your education on options with this book. Do more extensive research so that you can identify the best opportunities for you. Doing this will allow you to form the best strategy for your case and goals. Do not skip doing your homework because you are eager. Jumping the gun has led to many traders losing out. You need to rule your desires, wants, and actions rather than being ruled by them.
- **Being Committed.** A successful options trader is one that does not give up. He or she does not trade on an on-again, off-again basis. This person is committed to the cause of building their financial success in this way and persists in their effort. This is

something you embrace as a business and part of your lifestyle. Go hard or go home. Options trading has no room for being tentative.

- **Continually learning.** The financial market is continuously evolving. It changes every single day. A good trader needs to have a strong view of what is happening now and be able to roll with the punches. He or she also wants to be able to make assumptions about the future. Continuously learning about the market also allows you to see new opportunities where amateur traders will not. Following the behavior of an experienced options trader, is one of the best ways to increase your awareness of options. The point is not to copy his or her moves. Rather, it is to watch a master at work so that you can develop your own style of trading.

- **Being patient.** This relates to jumping the gun. Before you make a move when trading options, you need to consider your options carefully. While there are risks involved in trading options, the market typically provides signs of these opportunities if a trader knows where and how to look. Control your emotions and strategize your entry into the trade market as well as your exit from trades.

- **Being an effective risk manager.** There is no guarantee when you trade options, and as such, an effective options trader needs to be able to exploit his or her position to try to determine where he or she should take appropriate measures to capitalize on his or her gain. Part of managing risks involves being able to diversify your portfolio so that all your eggs are not in one basket. A successful trader does not go chasing after every available option. Neither does he or she get stuck chasing China eggs that do not yield gain. While there is no assurance that all will work out, being able to handle risks efficiently greatly decreases the chances of losses occurring.

- **Being able to manage money effectively.** The trader also needs to know how much capital should be allocated for trading. Throwing your money at all options will not lead to effective results. Actually, this is a recipe for losing money. Part of being a good money manager means the trader needs to be good with numbers such that he/she can calculate the vega, theta, delta, and gamma of their trade options, for example.

- **Maintaining accurate records.** This will help with decision-making and allows you to allocate your money effectively as you will have a history of your options within easy reach. My suggestion is that you do this digitally for easy access, better storage, and better organization. Digitally record-keeping also allows for the use of specialized software that makes life a lot simpler than looking through hard copies when records are needed.

- **Being an effective planner.** While there is a level of relying on instinct in trading options, you also need to have a plan so you do not place random trades. You need to have the direction to effectively move forward with obtaining financial freedom no matter which option you choose to do that. Having smart goals allow you to develop this plan. You also need to have a plan to cover any losses that may happen and a plan for how you can leverage the profit that you do make. Your plan needs to allow for flexibility, and the great thing is that you can upgrade, downscale, and change the plan completely if need be.

- **Being able to accept losses gracefully.** The nature of the financial market is unpredictable, and every trader makes a loss at some point. Having an apt understanding of the market will minimize this loss, but you also need to be able to be flexible in how you handle this so that you do not get blindsided, nor do you let this weigh you down. Remember that any successful person needs to be able to find a lesson in their failure o that they will come back in the future stronger and better.

Dream Big

Many people are stuck in a state of financial dependency and insecurity because they do not see themselves as being any better than they are now. Therefore, they never take any actions or risks to elevate themselves. You need to be able to visualize your success to manifest it. To develop yourself into a brilliant trader, you need to be able to see yourself in the future as a successful entrepreneur who implemented a plan to gain passive income and is, therefore, able to enjoy the freedom of using your time as you see fit.

The brain has a way of manifesting action to make what it sees a reality, so use that to your advantage. See yourself as a successful options trader today. Imagine the way that you would look, the way that you would feel, how you would dress and everything else that being an options trader means to you. See yourself being more than what you are today, no matter your current circumstances. Do not place any limits on yourself.

The mistake that many options traders make at the beginning is that they think small. They imagine maybe making a few hundred dollars here and there to subsidize their current lifestyle. They make that the pinnacle of their success even though many options traders make hundreds of thousands and millions of dollars every day.

The people that dream so small have their own reasons, but a common reason is that they do not want to be too disappointed if things do not work out. This way of thinking is limiting and self-fulfilling. You are stopping yourself from achieving greatness and reaching your true potential with such a mindset. Instead, you have to dream big, bold dreams. It is the only thing that will keep you motivated in tough times. You have to know that you can do this and make this a successful business no matter the odds.

I know that at the beginning, it may be tough, especially when people laugh at your dreams of becoming a success. Remember that you are not doing this for them. Those people may be your friends and family, and of course, this hurts. Do not allow this to demotivate you. Keep strong and remember that you are doing this for yourself, not them. If you need to, make it an extra motivator to prove them wrong. Give yourself the last laugh.

Visualizing allows you to have something to work towards. The vision creates a hunger within you to manifest that picture in your mind into reality. It builds anticipation and creates excitement. It gives you a sense of purpose. Allow yourself to be consumed by that passion.

My belief is that every person on this planet is capable of doing great things, so stop limiting yourself. Stop underestimating your potential. The willingness to follow his or her gut is one of the most essential characteristics of an options trader. You will never develop that knack for trading options if you continually doubt yourself and your purpose. All of the traits that are stated above are things that can be learned. So it is fine if you have not developed these traits as yet. The point is to make it a habit to develop them starting today. The first thing you need to do is picture yourself as the successful options trader that you will be in the future. Then put in the work to make that vision a reality.

Chapter 2. What an Option Is and Types

There are several types of options that are commonly traded. These options can be categorized into various forms concerning the features they possess. The broad sense of options has two major types of options. The two options are known as puts and call options. A call option can give a buyer the right to purchase a financial instrument. On the other hand, options hand an individual the right to sell the asset. There is a clear distinction that is used to classify the option, which is it's either they are European-style or American-style. The notion you can end up having is that the classification is done based on geographical location, which is not the case. The factual truth is that the classification is done because of where the contract has the potential of being exercised.

The process of classification of the option goes a notch further to using the method used in trading to classify them. Other methods used to distinguish the existing types of options include the underlying security they relate to and the expiration cycle that they contain. This broadens individual findings to several types of options that exist across the globe. These types of options can be well expounded for an individual to understand the concept of trade options. They include:

Calls Options

These types of options are characterized by giving an individual the right to purchase the agreed asset on a future date. The assets being purchased tend to have an already agreed-upon price. Certain situations can make an individual make a call on an asset. The most common situation is when one speculates that the asset will improve in its worth over a certain time. A characteristic of calls is that they have an expiry date, which is dependent on the contract a person has entered. The asset being targeted can be bought before the expiration date.

Puts Options

Puts are always the exact opposite of calls kind of options. An individual who owns the put option has the right bestowed to him of selling the underlying assets. The process of selling tends to have an agreed price that has been determined for the future act. This scenario happens during intriguing phases in the financial markets. An individual is likely to fall under put action when he or she has speculated the value of the assets to fall. Despite being the opposite of the call, there are similarities between calls and puts. A similar major occurrence is that they are both limited to the time set. Therefore, puts have an expiration date on the contract one has entered.

American-Style Options

The American-style has nothing related to buying and selling of contracts when it narrows down to options. It focuses its lenses on the terms that are stated in the contractual terms in an agreement. Basic knowledge at this point is that options come with an expiration date in their contracts, which gives a trader in the financial markets the right of either buying or selling an underlying asset. In the American-style option, an individual has the right to exercise his or her contract before the expiration date in the contract. The stated flexibility tends to advantage to a trader using American-style options.

European-Style Options

Individuals who are afforded this type of option are not given the same flexibility that is experienced by people who are using American-style contracts. The timeline in this type of option is very strict. An individual using European-style contracts is supposed to only trade his or her underlying assets on the expiration date and not before or after.

Exchange-Traded Options

It is also commonly known as listed options across the globe to several financial market participants. It can be considered as one of the most common types of options known to people. Several option contracts are listed on the public trading exchanges. These are the kinds of options that are referred to as exchange trade options. They can be able to be bought or sold by anyone with the aid of subtle brokers.

Over the Counter Options

This kind of trade option is only traded in the over-the-counter markets. These common characteristics that compound over-the-counter trade options make them not easily accessible to the entirety of the public. The terms of contracts in these forms of trade options tend to be complicated compared to other forms of trade options.

Employee Stock Options

This form of stock options is known to be presented to employees. An employee of a certain company offering options can be granted this contract by the company he/she is working for. Their general use is to facilitate remuneration to employees. It goes ahead to act as bonuses or incentives employees of a specific company are given. It has several advantages since it attracts people to work for organizations that offer such.

Cash Settled Options

These kinds of contracts do not characterize themselves with the physical transfer of the traded assets. What is takes place in a cash-settled option can be related to the name it possesses. Profits that are made in this kind of option are settled in cash forms to the winning party. Certain reasons befall this type of options trading. It comes to the occurrence when the asset being transferred is expensive or complicated to be transferred to the other party.

Types of Options Based on Expiration

Contracts have the possibility of being classified according to their expiration dates. This relates to certain phenomena that a trader is supposed to be able to sell concerning the set date in a contract. The contacts agreed that options trading tends to differ with the cycles they possess. They include:

- **Regular Options:** these are based on the cycles the trade is agreed upon and listed in the contracts. One is likely to have four expiration months to choose from in a financial year.
- **Weekly Options:** They were introduced in the year 2005 and are also known as weeklies. They have the same principles as regular options though they had reduced timings in them. Weeklies tend to be used in limited financial instruments.
- **Quarterly Options:** They are listed in the exchange markets, with their expiration dates being similar or near to financial quarters. Some people term them as weeklies, and they expire on the last day of expiration.

Types of Options by the Underlying Security

A stock option is a general that has been the focus when people tend to talk about trade options. This is where the underlying assets of the accompanying are publicly listed can be used as a financial instrument. It is common knowledge of people who have invested in this form of trade. There are several kinds of options that are involved in this case, and they include:

- **Stock Options:** A company that is publicly listed has its shares is; they form underlying assets that are being traded in this contract.
- **Index Options:** They tend to have a close similarity to the stock options. However, there is a difference that depicts the blurred line. The split comes when the underlying form of security being traded is not stocks; rather. They are a company's indexes.
- **Currency Options:** This contract has a clear difference from other forms of option. It is because it gives a trader the right to either sell or buy currency. The trade is made at the agreed terms of the contract.
- **Future Options:** The future contract is the underlying asset used in this form of options trading. A future Option has the potential of giving a trader a right to participate in a future contract.
- **Commodity Option:** The asset which is underlined in this kind of options trading tends to be a physical commodity.
- **Basket Option:** It is a kind of options trading that has several financial instruments as the underlying assets.

Exotic Options

It is a term that is used to characterize those options contracts that have been customized by options traders. The effect of this customization makes the contracts to be more complex. They are termed as Non-Standardized options in some cases. They are additional exotic contracts that are only found in the OTC markets. However, there are some of these options contracts that have started being famous in the current financial markets. These options include:

- **Barrier Options:** a pay-out is always given to a holder of this form of the contract until the moment the price stated in this contract reaches.
- **Binary Options:** the owner of the underlying financial assets is given a fixed amount of money in the event the contract expires.
- **Chooser Options:** these form of trade options allows a financial trader to choose whether to call or put at any time.
- **Compound Options:** a form of trading option in which the underlying financial asset is another option.

Chapter 3. How to Get Started in Options Trading

Determine Whether You Will Proceed as a Company or an Individual

Both these alternatives are a lot different when actual options trading comes into practice. The legal obligations of both vary significantly. Besides, check whether you can trade with an offshore company and/or an offshore bank account. This could be advantageous in some tax-related situations. Non-resident citizen offshore companies and bank accounts are quite beneficial.

Open a Trading Account

Setting up an online trading account is the foremost thing to do when starting trading in options. Step-by-step instructions are provided by companies, which makes it extremely easy to manage the account. Start early because this process might take a while. A lot of factors are taken into consideration while deciding on your trading account. The amount of money you are planning to invest in is the first thing that defines the type of account, which will be opened.

Another choice one may get if they want to open a margin account or not. A Margin account has its own benefits.

After selling a stock or option, you get the money immediately, which in turn enables you to buy again. Some time is required in a regular account to clear the proceeds from a sale. A Margin Account enables you to borrow money to trade while using your own capital at the same time. One can say that it is like an overdraft facility, which allows you to get extra funds.

Create a Plan

The idea of the matter is that there is simply no way you can expect to be successful in the long term when it comes to options trading if you don't have a plan that has been personalized based on your very own strengths and weaknesses. While skipping this and finding a generalized trading plan online may be the fastest way to start trading options as soon as possible, it is far from the most efficient.

Determine Your Current Level of Skill

To ensure that you create a plan with a realistic chance for success, the first thing that you would want to do is determine what your current competencies are when it comes to trading in general and the underlying asset you are hoping to focus on specifically. The more experience you have, the more elaborate and ambitious your plan can be, but it is important to determine your level of experience honestly, as overestimating your experience is only going to make it harder for you to start turning a profit in the first place.

Consider Other Obstacles

While you will likely have a few personal issues that may need to be worked through to achieve options trading success, it is important to also consider any other obstacles that might be standing in your way so that you can approach them properly. These obstacles can be anything from the limited amount of time that you are ultimately going to have to work with to simply not having the level of capital you would prefer to get started in the most effective way possible. It does not matter what the barrier is, it only matters how you are going to circumvent it. Having a clear idea of what may get in the way of your future success will allow you to prepare for it ahead of time and mitigate its long-term impact as much as possible. Taking the time to work through this step properly will help improve not only your overall success rate but your bankable profits as well.

Decide the Risk That Is Right for You

When it comes to determining how much risk is the right amount, the final solution is going to be different for each trader. This is because there is no singular amount of risk that is perfect for everyone; the risk is more individualized than that. To get started figuring out the perfect amount of the risk for you, the first thing that you will want to do is to determine how much capital you are going to allot solely to trading, as well as what that amount means to you. If you have saved a few thousand dollars in a month or so to give something new a try, then your overall risk is going to be low. If you saved that same amount over nearly a year of dedicated saving, then that same amount might represent a much higher risk. Regardless, it is important to never put more into a single trade than you can ever afford to lose.

Prepare Yourself

In addition to the daily preparations that will be required of you, you will also need to be aware of various important due dates, both for your underlying asset of choice as a whole, as well as any holdings you might have specifically. Earnings reports of all types are sure to have a noticeable effect on the market, and if you are caught unaware, you have no choice but to take a loss that, in many cases, can be quite serious. You would also need to be mindful of when any dividend payments are coming due for any options that are related to stocks that you might own. Owning an option does not entitle you to a dividend so, you must know when to exercise your options if you always hope to maximize your profits.

Find the Right Place to Start

Once you know when you are going to get out of any trade that you place, the succeeding thing that you will need to consider is the right time to capitalize on the trend of a specific option. The greatest way to go about doing this is to consider the amount of risk that you deem acceptable before considering what type of purchase you want to make when you come across an option that meets your criteria for purchase based on your earnings goals and your risk assessment.

Set Clear Goals

You are going to want to ensure that the goals you set are specific, which means setting goals with clear instances of success and failure for three months, six months and a year down the line. Having a strict timeline will make it easier for you to follow through on your goals, as you know exactly when you will have failed if you do not get to work. This means you will want to carefully consider all the logistics related to meeting your goals, as well as anything that may be standing between you and completing the goal successfully. Remember, the more specific you are when it comes to setting your goals, the more likely you are to achieve them. Don't forget that there is nothing more important than having a timeline set up from the get-go, as if your goals do not have timeframes, then it will be much easier to put them off overall.

Keep Track of Your Progress

When you are first making your way into the world of options trading, you must track your progress to ensure that you do not start on the wrong foot. This means you will want to track all the details of each trade that you make for closer analysis. Depending on how useful you find this process early on, you may even want to continue it into the foreseeable future. This means that you would want to track the time and date of each trade, the relevant financial specifics, why you choose the option in question, your emotional state, how long you held the option for, and the end result of the trade.

The First Trade

Once you have a firm trading plan in mind, there is nothing else to do except to put your plan to the test and see how things shake out in the real world. Though there are plenty of possibilities out there for you to practice trading before you get started doing the real thing, the fact of the matter is that if a real money isn't on the line, then you are going to inherently be in a different mental space about the entire thing which, by and large, will make the entire exercise moot. As such, it is recommended that you instead simply start by making trades that are at less than one percent of your total trading amount so that you aren't hobbled by high stakes while still not being in any real danger should things not go according to plan.

Making a Trade

When the time comes to make your first trade, you will want to select Trading Options from inside your trading account after you have already logged in. This will take you to a page that will allow you to search for various stock market options based on the ticker symbol of various underlying stocks. A search of a specific company will provide you with the current stock price as well as all the options related to the stock in question that are currently available.

Taking a Closer Look at Your Results

While it is perfectly natural to be curious as to the results of your personalized trading plan, remember that if you check in on your results too early, the available data is unlikely to be telling the whole story; to put it another way, you need to give you plan time to breathe before looking for hard and firm results.

What's more, if these early risky moves do work out, then you have negative trading habits to contend with that are sure to hamper your overall earnings potential further down the line. Instead of setting this type of largely irrelevant and frequently damaging goals, you are going to want to simply keep track of all the details without interacting with them until the time is right.

When it comes to tracking your trades properly, the strongest metric for success is going to vary noticeably depending on what types of trades you tend to prefer. If you find yourself constantly making risky trades that may pay off significantly, then you will be most interested in the pure amount you have made overall while day trading. However, if you are a trader that prefers to take things at a more cautious pace, then you will be interested more in the number of trades you have completed that ended successfully versus the number that ended in a loss as a pure number might not tell the whole story in that case. Do not forget to consider which metrics are right for you, as basing your analysis on the wrong data could easily send you spiraling in a counterproductive situation when you were already on the right track, to begin with.

Measure Your Performance

After you have amassed the appropriate amount of information, the succeeding thing you will want to do is to chart out your current overall performance. Doing so will provide you with an unbiased look at how all the rules you are using to properly determine your trades are doing without any of the daily, in-the-moment clutter getting in the way. Ideally, this data will include the results of each trade that you have made since you started options trading. Looking at all the data splayed out in this way will make it much easier to see the whole instead of the individual things.

Chapter 4. Options Strategies

Long Straddle

In a long straddle, you'll simultaneously buy a put and call for the same underlying stock. You're also going to want the same strike price and expiration date. This technique is something that can be utilized with a highly volatile stock. That way, you have the possibility of profiting no matter which way the stock moves. Before we see how this works, let's step back for a second and recall how we determine whether or not a deal is going to be profitable. We are looking at this from the buyer's perspective.

In a call option, you're going to profit when the stock exceeds the strike price. However, you must remember to include the premium in your calculation. If you think a stock will go higher than $54, but you're paying a $1 premium per share, then you will have to invest in a call option that has a strike price of at least $55.

In a put option, it's the same game, but you're hoping the stock will go below the strike price. So, for our new scenario of buying a call and a put at the same strike price and expiration date, we will buy a put with a strike price of $55. For simplicity, we will stay with a $1 premium.

Now you need to know the net premium, which will be the sum of the premium from the call option + the premium from the put option, in this case, $2.

You can get a profit when one of two conditions are met:

- Price of underlying stock > (Strike price of call + Net Premium). In our example, you will make a profit when the amount of the underlying stock is higher than $55 + $2 = $57.
- Price of underlying stock < (Strike price of put – Net Premium). Using our example, you'll see a profit when the price of the underlying stock is less than $55- $2 = $53.

The maximum loss for a straddle will occur when the contract expires with the underlying trading at the strike price. In that case, both contracts expire, and you're out the premiums paid for both options.

A long straddle has two break-even points. These are:

- Lower break-even point: Strike price – Net premium
- Upper break-even point: Strike price + Net premium

Remember you buy both options with the same strike price and expiration date.

Let's look at a simple example. A stock is trading at $100 a share in May. The investor buys a call with a strike price of $200 that expires on the third Friday in June for $100. The investor also buys a put with a strike price of $200 that expires on the third Friday of June for $100.

The net premium is $100 + $100 = $200.

Now suppose that on the expiry date, the stock is trading at $300. The put expires as worthless since the stock price of the underlying is far above the strike price of the put. However, the investor's call option expires in the money with an intrinsic value of 100 x ($300 - $200) = $10,000. Less the premium, the investor has made $9,800.

On the other hand, suppose that the stock drops in value, and on the expiry, is trading at $50. This time, the call option expires as worthless. The investor can buy 100 shares at a price of $50 each for a total cost of $5,000. Now he can sell them to exercise the put option at $200 a share, so he nets $20,000 - $5,000 - $200 = $14,800.

This is a fictitious example, so whether the numbers are realistic or not really isn't the point – the point is that the investor will profit no matter what happens to the stock price.

Strangle

The term strangle is an adaptation of the straddle. In this case, you also simultaneously buy a call option and a put option. However, instead of buying them at the same strike price, you buy them at different strike prices. For this type of strategy, you will buy slightly out-of-money options. This is used when you think that the underlying stock will undergo significant volatility in the short term. You will achieve a profit with a strangle when one of two conditions are met:

- Price of underlying stock > (strike price of call + Net Premium paid) or
- Price of underlying stock < (strike price of put – Net premium paid)

Usually, the strike price of the put is set at a lower value. Profit is determined by one of two possibilities:

- Profit = Price of underlying stock – strike price of call – net premium
- Profit = Strike price of put – the price of underlying stock – net premium

Bear Spread

A bear spread is profitable when the underlying stock price declines. Like the above strategies, a bear spread involves the simultaneous purchase of more than one option; however, in a bear spread, you buy two options of the same type. Alternatively, a call bear spread involves selling a call with a low strike price and buying a call with a high strike price.

Bull Spread

A bull spread is designed to profit when the price of the underlying security has a modest price increase. You can do a bull spread using either call or put options.

Married Puts

A married put is basically an insurance policy like that we described earlier. You buy a stock and a put option at the same time in order to protect yourself against possible losses from the stock.

Cash Secured Puts

In a cash-secured put, you secure the possible purchase of stock by having money in your brokerage account to cover the purchase. This will allow you to purchase stock at a discount, provided you have enough money in your account to actually buy the stock. In short, you write a put option and set aside the cash to purchase the stock. Cash secured put is done when you are bullish on the underlying stock but believe it will undergo a temporary downturn.

Rolling

Rolling a trade simply means that you are simultaneously closing out your existing positions and opening new ones based on the same underlying stock. When rolling a position, you can change the strike price, the duration of the contract, or both. You can roll forward, which means to extend the expiration date for the option.

A roll-up means that you increase the strike price when you open the new contract. A roll-up is used on a call option when you believe the underlying stock is going to increase in price. When you are trading put options, you use a roll down. In that case, you close your option and reopen it with the same underlying stock but with a lower strike price. A higher strike price means that the new position will be cheaper. When rolling, you're going out in time to the deadline. When rolling a call, you're hoping that the stock will rise in price. In this case, you're rolling to an out-of-the-money position. The price of the new call will drop. With a put, the opposite occurs, and the price of the new put will increase.

Chapter 5. How to Maximize Profits

Monitoring the Trend

Trends are a graphical measure of the actual activities that are taking place in the day trading market.

Any trader closely following up the trend makes him, or her informed and accurate in his or her levels of predictions, and chances are that winning may be their middle name. They are able to purchase when the prices are high and short sell when they drop. Analyzing trends has several assumptions in that if there are continuous cases of rising prices, possibilities are that they will constantly happen and vice versa.

News on Trading

News always comes in two ways; good news and bad news. Well, good news on day trading always gives the traders and brokers a huge motivation to purchase prices at good rates. When it comes to bad news, on the other hand, the traders are given an opportunity to short sell prices. This kind of strategy can be used as a great move in making huge amounts of profits at a particular season and induce high volatility rates.

Scalping

Scalping takes advantage of the small kind of prices that happen drastically during the day trading sessions. This kind of mechanism involves getting engaged so quickly and so fast and then leaving right away.

Contrarian Investing

This kind of strategy describes the assumption that prices will go up and most probably reverse and then drop. The contrarian buys during fall or short sell during the rise periods. The attitude in this kind of strategy defines that the whole expectation idea is to subdue to change and that things are to head in a reverse kind of direction.

Financial Management

Capital is so lucrative in any kind of income-generating activity. There are always going to be several wins and losses. Not to sound so risky, most of the traders will not input 2% of their capital in any line of trade. Be careful in whatever you consider as an investment; money loss is ever an option too.

Also, there may be cases where brokers demand high rates of commissions, do not fall into that trap. That is going to cause you big time. Consider the rates of commissions demanded by brokers in the first place because too many expenses in commissions can definitely incur low rates of profits, basically meaning that losses will be incurred.

Proper Time Management

Day trading is a journey. A certain market trading journey, meaning that for it to be called a journey, a particular process is established. A certain planned time span is encouraged. Monitor everyday trading move that occurs and will occur for it makes you learn and experience all about day trading. Good things take time; mastering the day trading occurrences is quite an investment. Remember, those good investments imply good rates of profits.

Consistency/ Stability

Another point to add, day trading is quite logical. Day trading cannot be analyzed by fear or even greed. Mathematical approaches have to be considered. Set strategies have to be put in place too! Examine every logical operation bound to happen during day trading so as to possess certain clear stability. Once stability has been established, expect some big-time profit rates and an excellent reputation.

Timing

The trading market becomes volatile every single trading day. Experienced traders have mastered the moves, and so they are quite sure about what steps to take once they get to read the structures. As a beginner, do not be quite in a rush to predict. Take one or more time to examine every single trend and get your desired prediction. Do not be too slow though, you may end missing so much.

Momentum

This kind of strategy defines revolving around new sources and also identifying the substantial trending moves at a high stake. You basically should basically maintain your current position, be alert with the reversing signs and face a totally different direction.

Strong Focus on One Particular Market

Many traders become overexcited and want to trade with all markets. This should not be the case; you will end up being confused, not knowing which trade to focus on. It is normally healthy for the business when you decide and focus on one trade, be good at it. Focusing on many trades at a go will make you lose.

Trading Pivots

Trading pivots come in when you buy low at the end of the day, and you sell at the high end of the trading day. Once you get to master these tactics, the chances are that you will be an expert in comprehending the volatility of the market and therefore declare yourself successful using this kind.

Risk Control

For beginners, it is highly recommended that they engage in trading infrequently as a way of avoiding too many risks. The essence of this is to help them master their moves and learn a lot. Day trading is not just about profits only; it is about taking each day as a learning trading progress. Predict the trends at least after some minutes and not just seconds. I am familiar with the adage that declares that, commit many mistakes to learn highly, but honey, this is some real cash being retrieved from your pocket; you can become poor any minute. Slow but sure steps are highly recommended. Take each trading day as a lesson. With this, tricks and knowledge are so equipped, and with no time, you will be so okay.

Passive Position Management

A novice day trader is prone to adjust their target and stops abruptly because of being controlled by certain emotions. These kinds of emotions are caused by the sudden updates of the figures and trends on the screen that keep changing with time. This is so confusing for the beginners and, after all causing them to alter their predictions hence leading to a great downfall. Only highly experienced and confident day traders can analyze the updates because they may actually know what they are doing.

For the novice day traders, leave the targets and the stops on their own, and learn how you would passively control all these. Reach for some paper material and sketch and assume how the aftermath would be without interfering with your active trends. Do some in-depth examination and comprehend why every move is happening. In the end, compare what you would have affected your trading account if at all you altered the last trends. This is a learning process. Do this for quite a while, and within no time, day trading becomes your all-time income-generating hobby. Yes!

Protect Your Capital

Losses are normally involved in almost all businesses; despite that, try your best and protect the capital of your business. This can be achieved by shunning all unnecessary risks that come along in businesses. This will definitely bring success to your business.

Risk reward ratio of 3:1

Comprehending the proper 3:1 risk-reward ratio is so important. This kind of ratio reward encourages a trader to lose small and then win big despite the frequent times you lost on the trading platform. The moment you gain some wide experience, the risk-reward ratio gets higher and higher, meaning that you are slowly advancing and enjoying some good profits. This is the kind of measure we need to strategize to grow as traders.

Patience and Persistence

Plan your trades before you trade your plans. This kind of strategy defines the behavior where most traders do not really trade daily. They have this kind of paradoxical behavior where they just check up on the trends without necessarily acting up because of the fear of outlining the wrong prediction. Well, this is not really a way of learning. Day trading calls for patience and persistence, where several wrongs did are part of the journey, and learning happens a lot through that. Carefully plan your trades and then predict, see how this goes. Be patient and persistent in every move you make. After all, good things always take time.

Hard Work

Day trading requires you to be hardworking to be successful. It is not like the entertainment business, which you can joke around with. It needs maximum practice in trading and discipline. You have to be trading frequently and stay updated on the stock price fluctuations.

The above strategies help to improve time factors, skills, financial management operations, to grow as a person, risk management and most importantly, you get to learn.

Chapter 6. Risk Management

Excellent risk management can save the worst trading strategy, but horrible risk management will sink even the best strategy. This is a lesson that many traders learn painfully over time, and I suggest you learn this by heart and install it deep within you even if you can't fully comprehend that statement.

Risk management has many different elements to both quantitative and qualitative. When it comes to options trading, the quantitative side is minimal thanks to the nature of options limiting risk by themselves. However, the qualitative side deserves much attention.

Risk

What is the risk at any rate? Logically, it is the probability of you losing all of your money. In trading terms, you can think of it as being the probability of your actions, putting you on a path to losing all of your capital. An excellent way to think about the need for proper risk management is to ask yourself what a lousy trader would do. Forget trading, what would a lousy business person do with their capital?

Well, they would spend it on useless stuff that adds nothing to the bottom line. They would also increase expenses, market poorly, not take care of their employees, and be undisciplined with regards to their processes. While trading, you don't have employees or marketing needs, so you don't need to worry about that.

Do you have suppliers and costs? Well, yes, you do. Your supplier is your broker, and you pay fees to execute your trades. That is the cost of access. In directional trading, you have high costs as well because taking losses is a necessary part of trading. With market-neutral or non-directional trading, your losses are going to be minimal, but you should still seek to minimize them.

What about discipline? Do you think you can trade and analyze the market thoroughly if you've just returned home from your job and are tired? If you didn't sleep properly last night, or if you've argued with your spouse or partner? The point I'm making is that the more you behave like a terrible business owner, the more you increase your risk of failure.

Odds and Averages

Trading requires you to think a bit differently about profitability. I spoke about minimizing costs, and your first thought must have been to seek to reduce losses and maximize wins. This is a natural product of linear or ordered thinking. The market, however, is chaotic, and linear thinking is going to get you nowhere.

Instead, you must think about averages and odds. Averages imply that you need to worry about your average loss size and your average win size. Seek to decrease the former and increase the latter. Notice that when we talk about averages, we're not necessarily talking about reducing the total number of losses. You can reduce the average by either reducing the sum of your losses or by increasing the number of losing trades while keeping the sum of the losses constant. This is a shift in thinking you must make.

Thinking in this way sets you up nicely to think in terms of odds because, in chaotic systems, all you can bank on are odds playing out in the long run. For example, if you flip a coin, do you know in advance whether it's going to be heads or tails? Probably not. But if someone asked you to predict the distribution of heads versus tails over 10,000 flips, you could reasonably guess that it'll be 5000 heads and 5000 tails. You might be off by a few flips either way, but you'll be pretty close percentage-wise.

The greater the number of flips, the lesser your error percentage will be. This is because the odds inherent in a pattern that occurs in a chaotic system express themselves best over the long run. Your trading strategy is precisely such a pattern. The market is a chaotic system. Hence, you should focus on executing your strategy as it is meant to be executed over and over again and worry about profitability only in the long run.

Contrast this with the usual attitude of traders who seek to win every single trade. This is impossible to accomplish since no trading strategy or pattern is correct 100% of the time.

This is because you don't have to do much when trading options. You enter and then monitor the trade. Sure, it helps to have some directional bias, but even if you get it wrong, your losses will be extremely limited, and you're more likely to hit winners than losers.

Despite this, always think of your strategy in terms of its odds. There are two basic metrics to measure this. The first is the win rate of your system. This is simply the percentage of winners you have. The second is your payout ratio, which is the average win size divided by the average loss size.

Together, these two metrics will determine how profitable your system is. Both of them play off one another, and a decrease in another usually meet an increase in one. It takes an extremely skillful trader to increase both simultaneously.

Risk per Trade

The quantitative side of risk management when it comes to options trading is lesser than what you need to take care of when trading directionally. However, this doesn't mean there's nothing to worry about. Perhaps your risk per trade is the most significant metric of them all. The risk per trade is what ultimately governs your profitability.

How much should you risk per trade? Common wisdom says that you should restrict this to 2% of your capital. For options trading purposes, this is perfectly fine. Once you build your skill and can see opportunities better, I'd suggest increasing it to a higher level.

A point that you must understand here is that you must keep your risk per trade consistent for it to have any effect. You might see an excellent setup and think that it has no chance of failure, but the truth is that you don't know how things will turn out. Even the prettiest setup has every chance of failing, and the ugliest setup you can think of may result in a profit. So never adjust your position size based on how something looks.

Calculating your position size for a trade is a pretty straightforward task. Every option's strategy will have a fixed maximum risk amount. Divide the capital risk by this amount, and that gives you your position size. Round the position size down to the whole number since you can only buy the whole number lots when it comes to contract sizes.

For example, let's say your maximum risk is $50 per lot on the trade. Your capital is $10,000. Your risk per trade is 2%. So, the amount you're risking on that trade is 2% of 10,000, which is $200. Divide this by 50, and you get 4. Hence, your position size is four contracts or 400 shares. (You'll buy the contracts, not the shares.)

Why is it important to keep your risk per trade consistent? Well, recall that your average win and loss size is important when it comes to determining your profitability. These, in conjunction with your strategy's success rate, determine how much money you'll make. If you keep shifting your risk amount per trade, you'll shift your win and loss sizes. You might argue that since it's an average, you can always adjust amounts to reflect an average.

My counter to that is, how would you know which trades to adjust in advance? You won't know which ones are going to be a win or a loss, so you won't know which trade sizes to adjust to meet the average. Hence, keep it consistent across all trades and let the math work for you.

Aside from risk per trade, there are some simple metrics you should keep track of as part of your quantitative risk management plan.

Drawdown

A drawdown refers to the reduction in capital your account experiences. Drawdowns by themselves always occur. The metrics you should be measuring are the maximum drawdown and recovery period. If you think of your account's balance as a curve, the maximum drawdown is the biggest peak to trough distance in dollars. The recovery period is the subsequent time it took for your account to make new equity high.

If your risk per trade is far too high, your max drawdown will be unacceptably high. For example, if you risk 10% per trade and lose two in a row, which is very likely, your drawdown is going to be 20%. This is an absurdly large hole to dig your way out. Consider that your capital has decreased by 20%, and the subsequent climb back up needs to be done on lesser capital.

This is why you need to keep your risk per trade low and in line with your strategy's success rate. The best way to manage drawdowns and limit the damage they cause is to put in place risk limits per day, week, and month. Even professional athletes who train to do one thing all the time have bad days, so it's unfair to expect yourself to be at 100% all the time.

These risk limits will take you out of the game when you're playing poorly. A daily risk limit is to prevent you from getting into a spiral of revenge trading. A good limit to stick to when starting is to stop trading if you experience three losses in a row. This is pretty unlikely with options trades to be, honest unless you screw up badly, but it's good to have a limit in place from a perspective of the discipline.

Next, aim for a maximum weekly drawdown limit of 5% and a monthly drawdown limit of 6-8%. These are pretty high limits, to be honest, and if you are a directional trader, these limits don't apply to you. Directional traders need to be a lot more conservative than option traders when it comes to risk.

Understand that these are hard stop limits. So, if your account has hit its monthly drawdown level within the first week, you must take a break for a month. Overtrading and a lack of reflection on progress can cause a lot of damage, and a drawdown is simply a reflection of that.

Qualitative Risk

Quantitative metrics aside, your ability to properly manage qualitative things in your life and trading will dictate a lot of your success. Prepare well, and you're likely to see progress. You need to see preparation as your responsibility. I mean, no one else can prepare for you, can they?

Chapter 7. Tips and Tricks

If you are interested in embarking on the journey of earning money through options trading, there are a few issues to address before getting on board. Here are some of them:

Know When to Go Off the Manuscript

While sticking to your plan, even when your emotions are telling you to ignore it, is the mark of a successful trader, this in no way means that you must blindly follow your plan 100 percent of the time. Without a doubt, you would get yourself in a situation from time to time where your plan is going to be rendered completely useless by something outside of your control. You must be mindful enough of your plan's weaknesses, as well as changing market conditions, to know when following your predetermined course of action is going to lead to failure instead of success. Knowing when the situation is changing versus when your emotions are trying to hold sway comes with practice, but even being aware of the disparity is a huge step in the right direction.

Avoid Trades That Are Out of the Money

While there are a few strategies out there that make it a point of picking up options that are currently out of the money, you can rest assured that they are most certainly the exception, not the rule. Remember, the options market is not like the traditional stock market, which means that even if you are trading options based on underlying stocks buying low and selling high is just not a viable strategy. If a call has dropped out of the money, there is generally less than a 10 percent chance that it will return to acceptable levels before it expires, which means that if you purchase these types of options, what you are doing is little better than gambling, and you can find ways to gamble with odds in your favor of much higher than 10 percent.

Never Get Started Without a Clear Plan for Entry and Exit

More important than setting entry and exit points, however, is using them, even when there is still the appearance of money on the table. One of the biggest hurdles that new options traders need to get over is the idea that you must squeeze every last cent out of every successful trade. The fact of the matter is that, as long as you have a profitable trading plan, then there will always be more profitable trades in the future, which means that instead of worrying about a small extra profit, you should be more concerned with protecting the profit that the trade has already netted you. While you may occasionally make some extra profit ignoring this advice, odds are you will lose far more than you gain as profits peak unexpectedly and begin dropping again before you can effectively pull the trigger.

Read

Read at least one manuscript per week. This technique will teach you a lot of things, especially secrets. It will also provide you with a deeper understanding of the risks and rewards involved.

Trade for Income Not Wealth

If you do this thinking that you will be getting returns at 120%, you should reconsider. While one or two investments may yield such returns, the vast majority of options will not.

Start With Enough Capital

The first thing you need to make sure you are set up with includes having ample money to assist you to get into the investment. Capital is the amount of money you can bring into your account to help pay for all of the transactions you choose, and if you end up taking a loss when trading, it can be used.

You should always leave a little bit of money in your trading account. This is going to help you out when you are in the middle of a trade and can make it easier for your broker to keep working on trades without having to worry about a delay while your fund's transfer.

Avoid the Really Big Risks

Good options traders don't like a ton of risk, and they don't understand why they should take a big gamble just so they can get a tiny chance at a big payday. Rather than going after things like this, they are going to work on some trades that are high gain but lower in risk.

Be Sure to Diversify

Diversification is of the utmost importance. Having a portfolio that is not adequately diversified is a rookie mistake; however, many professional investors prefer not to diversify because of the way money is run in the United States.

Try Not to Panic

People don't make money from panicking in stressful situations. You will always encounter better times to leave or make a move rather than moves brought about by nervousness or panic. This is the downfall of a lot of people who are interested in investing but can't seem to master the craft.

See the Positive About It and Find Opportunities

The following time you notice there is a situation with trading that has brought a lot of panic on, you should immediately take the opposing side. Some of the best trades you can make involve the trade having been cleared out from people panicking and using their market orders without understanding that the doors for exiting are not as large as they believe or assume.

This doesn't mean all of the merchandise that people leave out of panic is worth investing in over long periods. Usually, when the market or stocks get socked, there will be a bounce-back that lets you leave in a better position than you would have if you went along with what everyone else was doing when they left too fast.

Trade at the Right Times

Since you are going to learn how to avoid big risks when you are an options trader, you are going to learn how to be very careful about your timing when it comes to entering and exiting the market. You should have the ability to analyze the market the right way so that you can learn the best time to do both of those tasks. These investors have spent their time doing some research, and they know how to look at the big picture, rather than always calling up the broker and hoping that they can trust that person.

Learn How to Be Focused

There are a few individuals who think that trading options are super easy, and then they jump in and get frustrated by what they are dealing with. If you are not used to this kind of investment, it may seem a bit hard to deal with in the beginning.

If you find that you are a person who is not able to easily focus on the task that you need to, then it is easy to have trouble with options trading because you are missing out on things. A trader who can maintain their focus for a long time is more likely to get more out of this trading style.

Never Follow the Crowd

One of the bad habits that you can do is try to follow the crowd and hope that will work out well for you. Many beginners find it easy to look to the experts for advice, and then they will follow exactly what that expert says without doing any of their research or trusting their judgment. There is nothing wrong with having an expert's advice, but your plan is not going to be the same as theirs. You are the only one who has an idea of your limits and your goals, and while you can listen to the advice that others give you, it is important to think for yourself and pick out a plan that works for you.

Keep It as Simple as Possible

Options trading is a complicated market by definition. You do not need to perplex things any further. Keep your strategies as simple as possible, use the simplest technical analysis tools, and manage your money in the simplest way possible. The rest will fall in place on their own.

Do Not Overtrade

When you start dealing with inexpensive options, it will be very easy to lose track of what you are trading with. Keep the number of contracts at a manageable level.

Pay Attention to Rankings

Especially if you are dealing with spreads, and particularly if you are a novice. Qualification rankings are available to consult at all times. An option that is not ranked high is not a good option, and it will probably cost you money.

Be Consistent

You would want to have a good understanding of the pros and cons of the different stocks in question before you ever make any trade, as well as the best point to enter a trade and at which point you would want to leave the trade if things go badly, and also where you can exit if things actually go as well as you might expect. Once you have made a plan, it is important to stick with it even if your emotions are making a compelling argument for going in another direction instead. It is important to always trust in your plan as it was made during a period when you were thinking as rationally as possible; giving in to your emotions at this point is akin to gambling with your investments.

Keep the Mood of the Market in Mind at All Times

Fundamental and technical analysis is all well and good, but they will only take you so far before you run into instances where the market seems to balk at the logical choice and move off in an unexpected direction. This typically happens when the will of the market goes against the status quo thanks to an unexpected outpouring of support from traders who are thinking with their guts instead of their brains. The greatest way to go about doing this is to keep tabs on what the major players in your market of choice are up to, as this will typically act as a litmus test when it comes to the feelings of the market as a whole.

Chapter 8. Practical Examples and Strategies

If you set up with a dealer, and you have got your very own trading room ready to go, a successful plan would be needed. Day-trading techniques come in all shapes and sizes, some simple and others complex. Before we look at an example, there are a few critical components that will involve most techniques. When you transact using the internet, you can typically use charts and trends to forecast potential changes in prices. They are based on fundamental theory, that history is repeating itself, and you will find many a wealthy trader who wholeheartedly agrees with that assertion.

Your map will claim the latest selling options indicators. These vary from strategy to strategy, which includes the Put-Call Ratio Tracker Capital Flow Index Open Interest Relative Strength Index Bollinger Bands. You will find that it takes hard work and experience to exchange trends for options. You would need to smooth out any creases and try several different charts before you find one with numbers that paints a good picture.

Covered Call Options

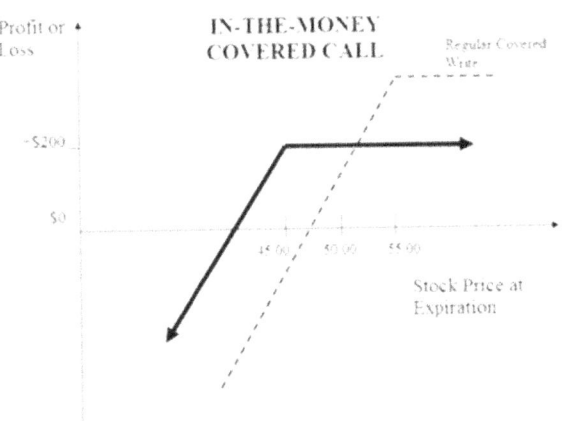

A call option is a contract option in which the holder (buyer) has the right (but not the obligation) to purchase a defined volume of a commodity at a predetermined date (strike price) within a given time (until its expiry).

This constitutes a duty for the writer (seller) of a call option to sell the underlying security at the strike price if the option is exercised. A prime is paid to the call choice writer for taking on the risk involved with the responsibility.

Each deal includes 100 shares, with stock options. The short call is protected if the writer of the call option owns the required amount of the security underlying it. The covered call is a common option technique that helps the stockholder to produce additional income from their stock holdings by periodic call options sales. For more info, please see our covered call strategy post. Someone should buy a bull call spread as an alternative to writing covered calls with a comparable benefit opportunity but with considerably less capital need. Instead of buying the underlying shares of the covered call strategy, the preferred bull call spread approach requires only that the trader purchase deep-in-the-money call options.

Because the aim of writing protected calls is to collect premiums, it makes sense to sell near-month options when time decay on those options is at its highest. Hence, the two tactics we equate would include selling marginally out-of-the-money call options in the near-month timeframe.

Married Put Options

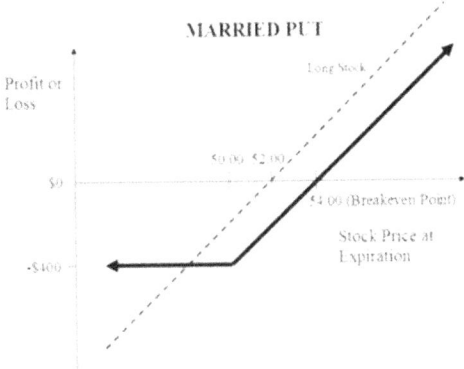

Both married put and long call have the same infinite benefit potential with no cap onto the underlying stock price appreciation. However, the benefit is often lower than just owning the stock, lowered by the cost or premium of the purchased option. Reaching break-even for strategy happens when the underlying stock increases by the number of premium options received. Anything beyond that is income.

The advantage of a married put is that the stock now has the floor minimizing downside risk. The floor is the difference between the underlying stock price, when the put was bought, and the put strike price. Simply put, when the option was acquired, if the underlying stock sold precisely at the strike price, the strategy loss is capped at exactly the price paid for the opportunity.

A married put is also called a long synthetic call, as it has the same profile. The strategy resembles purchasing a standard call option (without the underlying stock) because, for both, the same dynamic is real: limited risk, infinite profit potential. The difference between these approaches is clearly how much less money a long call takes.

Bull Call Spread Options

One may buy a bull call spread as an alternative to writing covered calls with a comparable benefit opportunity but with considerably less capital need. Because of purchasing the underlying stock of the covered call strategy, the preferred bull call spread approach requires only that the trader buy deep-in-the-money call options.

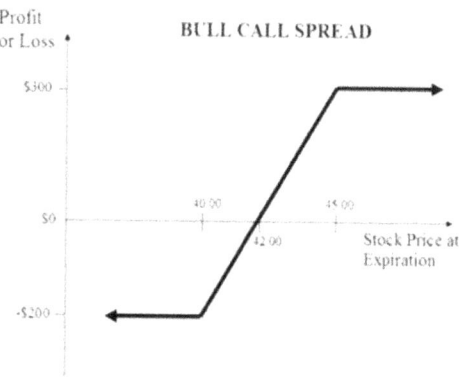

If the aim of writing protected calls is to collect premiums, it makes sense to sell near-month options when time decay for those options is at its highest. Hence, the two tactics we equate would include selling marginally out-of-the-money call options in the near-month period. The distribution of the bull call reduces the call option's risk, but it comes at a trade-off. The stock market returns are also capped, thereby having a small spectrum where the buyer will make a return. Traders will use the spread of the bull call as they expect the valuation of a commodity should increase moderately. Quite likely, they will use this technique at periods of high uncertainty.

The distribution of the bull call consists of steps that require two call options.

Pick the investments that you believe would grow over a given span of days, weeks, or months. Buy a call option on a particular closing date at a strike price above the selling rate and pay the premium. With this alternative, another name is a long call. Around the same time, sell a call option at a higher strike price and has the same expiry date as the first call option. Another term for a quick call for this alternative is.

Bear Put Spread Options

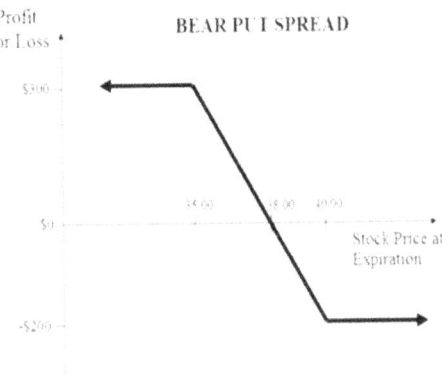

A bear put spread is a form of options strategy where an investor or trader expects a moderate downturn in security or asset prices. Bear put propagation is accomplished by purchasing put options when selling the same number of puts on the same security at the same expiry date at a lower strike price. With this method, the potential profit is the difference between the two strike costs, minus the options' net value.

For a note, an option is a right to sell a given quantity of underlying security at a defined strike price.

Often known as a debit put spread or a long-put spread. A bear put spread is an options technique executed by a bearish trader who aims to increase income while reducing profits.

A bear put spread approach entails purchasing and selling puts on the same underlying asset at the same expiry date but at different strike rates.

A bear puts spreads net profit as the price of the underlying security decreases. Therefore, net capital outlay is smaller than buying a single put outright. It also carries much less risk than shortening stock or protection, as the risk is limited to bear put spread net expense. Theoretically, selling a stock short has an infinite chance if the price goes higher. Unless the investor assumes the underlying stock or asset would decline by a small sum between the day of settlement and the expiry date, a bear put spread may be a perfect strategy. But, if the underlying stock or security declines by more than the dealer gives up the right to demand the extra Benefit. The trade-off between risk and future gain draws many traders.

Protective Collar Options

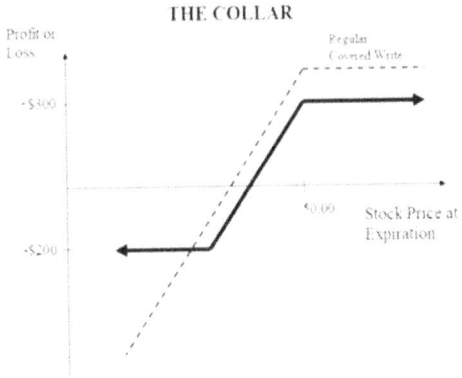

The protective collar technique is where you purchase some protection options, sell a short call option, and purchase a long-placed option to reduce downside risk. This technique defends stocks from low market values. It uses cash-on-call options when sold and a Put option when purchased.

Everyone else holds short securities, and the lender must pay the responsibility. Long Put Option is purchasing shares, assuming the stock price should be smaller than the expiry strike price. The investor holds the shares.

Fast call option – selling the current call option until the investor feels the market price would sink below the call strike point. The holder will benefit. Although the buyer will not own these shares, they must purchase them again later as the price falls and pay the owner.

Long and Short Strangle Options

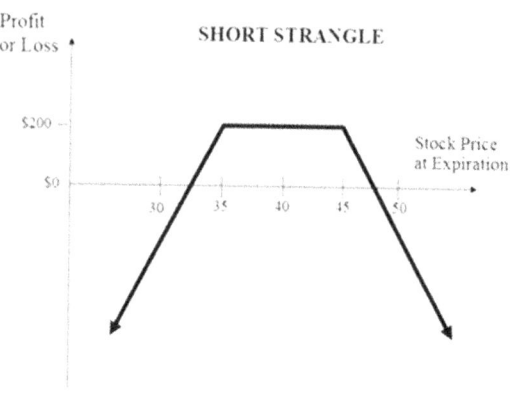

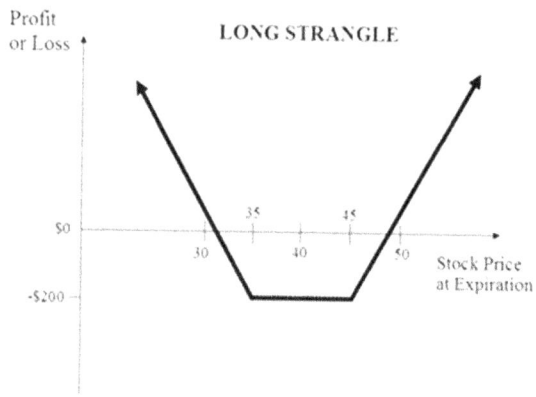

The endless options strangle a tremendous benefit, minimal risk approach that is taken while the dealer of the options considers the underlying stock and expiry date. Significant returns are obtained with the long strangle option strategy when the underlying stock price takes a very considerable step either upward or downward at expiry. The formula for estimating profit is given below:

Maximum Benefit = Unlimited Benefit Gained When Underlying Price > Long Call Strike Price + Net Premium Paid OR Underlying Price < Long Put Strike Price — Net Premium Paid Income = Underlying Price — Long

Call Strike Price — Net Premium Paid OR Long Put Strike Price — Underlying Price — Net Premium Paid.

A medium strangles one quick call with a higher trigger price and one low shot. All options have the same underlying supply and expiry date but different strike rates. If the underlying stock trades in a narrow range below the break-even points, a short strangle is formed for a net credit (or net receipt). Benefit opportunity is limited to cumulative contributions earning fewer commissions. Potential liability is infinite if stock demand increases and asset selling declines significantly. Full benefit efficiency is limited to overall fewer commissions earned. Total Benefit is gained if the short strangle expires, the stock price trades at or below strike rates, and all options expire worthlessly. The maximum probability of profit loss is infinite because the stock price can grow forever. The potential risk is significant on the downside when the stock price can fall to zero.

Chapter 9. Points of Interest for Options Trading

In stock option trading, there is more than just buying and selling contracts.

If you're thinking about going into trading or dabbling in it right now, here are some common issues that arise every day in trading stock options.

And these aren't merely questions of theory. At some point during your stock options trading career, each one represents a decision you will have to make. Answer wrong, and the odds are good that you will find yourself out of the money more times than you want to be.

Give a quick quiz to yourself. Do you know the best answer to the Top 12 Questions about Trading Options?

- When are you getting your premium? And does your premium receipt mean that you are in the money?
- Should your broker charge you interest when you write Puts? If you write Puts?
- What are the Naked Puts and Covered Calls differences?
- Is there a reason why you should write Covered Calls instead of Naked Puts?
- When should you write Secured Puts for Cash? And when do you ever have to write to them?
- When selling Covered Calls, how do you factor in Time Decay?
- What's the best stock options strategy for Naked Puts hedging?
- Should you ever close the Early Naked Put?
- What's the best stock options strategy for stop-loss trading?
- Does re-investing dividends make sense?
- How does your cost basis affect reinvested dividends?

- What type of trading strategy includes the sale of Covered Puts?

All of the questions have answers that are simple but significant. And what makes the difference between an options trading expert and someone who is simply throwing money into the market and hoping for the best is knowing those answers.

Several traders love to use more sophisticated options strategies in their trading, but the fairest trade for the market situation is the simple call options trade. To increase your likelihood of profiting from call option trading, follow the steps below.

1. Determine that the price is going up for the underlying instrument. Call options trading is a directional strategy. This means that you have to choose the market direction, and the market should move up to profit. There are many different ways in which upward market movement can be anticipated. Some individuals react to good market news, and some use basic data such as increasing profits per share, increasing revenue, increasing dividend yield, etc. Some use chart patterns, such as the double bottom, reverse head, shoulder, ascending triangle, and upside price breakout, to indicate upward market movement. Some utilize other systems, such as Elliot waves, and systems that use price pattern combinations and other indicators.

2. Determine the price movement's target. A target price for the activity should also be indicated by the system that you use to show an upward price movement.

3. To move to your target price, anticipate the time for the underlying price. How long do you expect the cost of the underlying tools to move to the target price? To determine the expiry of the call options you wish to trade, this is essential.

4. Look at the string of options. To see the prices and other relevant data, bring out the options chains. Nowadays, chains of real-time options are easily accessible through the internet. To get this information, you can also call your broker.

5. Narrow down to the date of exchange and expiry. If you trade online, determine the business to be submitted for your order. Based on the time you expect the price to change, choose a suitable expiration date. Usually, unless you use a trading system that trades options near their expiry, you would like to buy call options with an expiry that is slightly longer than the expected time. This fact is to decrease the effect of time decay. This fact is very significant because time decay can lead to a loss of value for your call options.

6. For several strike rates of the same expiry, compare the Delta, Gamma, Vega, and Theta. After you have narrowed down your options chain to the specific exchange and specific expiration date, you look at the Greeks. Ideally, you would like to have high Delta, high Gamma, low Vega, and low Theta. When the underlying instrument's price moves up, High Delta and High Gamma can give you a more significant and faster profit. Low Vega is very critical when you're buying options. Low Vega implies cheaper options, and you make profits even if the underlying price does not move when Vega increases. The low volatility and quiet market are associated with Low Vega. And Low Theta means that due to time decay, the call option causes smaller losses. You can choose out-of-the-money call options if you are a longer-term trader. Such alternatives have a smaller delta but are cheaper. If you are a shorter-term trader because they can give you faster and higher profits due to higher Delta and Gamma, you would prefer at-the-money or in-the-money call options.

7. Based on your target price, assess your risk versus rewards. You can also use a risk profile to assist you in making the assessment. Use this formula to calculate the breakeven point: breakeven = call strike + call premium.
8. Look at the interest and volume that is open. In an active market, it is better to trade so that you can easily purchase and sell. Another reason is that on the bid/ask spread, and you don't lose a lot.
9. Select the best option for the call with the highest profit probability.
10. Determine the exit point and prevent loss. Before you place in your trade, make sure you have your profit-taking points and stop-loss points in place. Do this so that your emotions do not take over your decision-making after you put in your trade.
11. Place your trade-in. Call your broker online or key in your trade.
12. Watch the price movement of the underlying instrument and the price response of the option.
13. Close your stance. If you have made a profit, close your position by either selling your purchased call options or exercising the call option and selling the shares. It is usually better to sell the call options if there is some time remaining before expiry because there is still time value. If you have made a loss by selling the call options, close your position.

Credit Diffusion Strategy

If you have been options trading for a bit, you may have come across a credit spread strategy for one option. Somehow, credit spread appears to be a popular strategy because it has been touted as a means for traders to consistently make money from the market by taking advantage of time decay.

At this point, I think it is crucial to align our understanding of the credit spread to avoid doubt. So what is the spread of credit? It is essentially an options strategy to be developed with the same expiration month by either using put options or call options. "This approach is part of the family of "vertical spread."

If a trader is bullish on the underlying stock or index, at a higher strike, he/she may sell a put option and buy a put option at the same time at a lower strike with the same expiration month. Conversely, if a trader is bearish on the underlying stock or index at a lower strike, he/she may sell a call option and purchase a call option at the same time at a higher strike with the same month of expiration.

Based on my coaching experience, the ideas of trading credit spreads fascinated quite a number of them because they seem to believe that their brokers would pay them for initiating new credit spreads. It sounds like "risk-free trades," doesn't it? This way is partly due to the word "credit," which indicates that a trader can receive free money from his/her brokers in the above context.

Sadly, this is not the case because there is no such thing called a credit spread in the options world known by market makers. There is no free lunch, and when initiating a new options position, no traders will be paid. In reality, if I were to use "credit spread," my mentors would scold me because the correct terminology for them is "selling a put spread." Suppose we are bullish on the underlying stock or index or "selling a call spread" if we are bearish on the underlying stock or index.

What's my point here? In reality, the answer is that a credit spread is a debit spread and a credit spread is a debit spread. No brokers will pay their customers to sell a call spread or a put spread (and that means other traders and me). The truth is that if it goes dead wrong, our brokers will charge us a margin that substantially represents the maximum risk of the spread.

Did you hear about the synthetic connection in the trading of options? You should, if not. It is possible to construct all "credit" put/call synthetically spreads as "debit" call/ put spreads because of the artificial relationship. Let us use a hypothetical stock - XYZ, currently trading at $360 per share, to go through the following example.

Suppose, on XYZ; we're bullish. A 355-350 put spread (i.e., selling 1 x 355 set and buying 1 x 350 put simultaneously) can be sold at, say, $0.60. In this case, the maximum trade reward is $0.60 with a $4.40 (i.e., $5.00 - $0.60) margin. Due to the synthetic relationship, by buying a 350-355 call spread (i.e., buying 1 x 350 call and simultaneously selling 1 x 355 call) for $ 4.40, we should create the same position, which means that the maximum reward will be $ 0.60.

Chapter 10. Rules for Successful Trading

Ensuring dependable profits in the financial markets is much more difficult than it seems at first glance. It is assessed that over 75% of all members, in the end, wash out and take up more secure side interests. Be that as it may, the financier business once in a while distributes customer disappointment rates since they're concerned reality may drive away new records, so the washout rate could be a lot higher.

The Road to Long-Term Profitability

Long-haul benefit requires two interrelated ranges of abilities. To begin with, we need techniques that get more cash-flow than they lose. Second, those techniques must perform well while the market shape-moves through bull and bear driving forces, with a lot of uneven periods in the middle. While numerous brokers realize how to profit in explicit economic situations, similar to a solid upturn, they bomb over the long haul on the grounds that their techniques don't adjust to unavoidable changes.

So would you be able to split away from the pack and unite the expert minority with a methodology that raises your chances for long-haul success? Begin with an unmistakable and succinct arrangement.

1. Disregard the Holy Grail

Losing brokers fantasize about the mystery recipe that will mysteriously improve their outcomes. As a general rule, there are no mysteries in light of the fact that the way to progress consistently goes through cautious decisions, viable risks the executives, and gifted benefit taking.

2. Connect with Your Trading Plan

Update your trading plan week by week or month to month to incorporate new thoughts and kill awful ones. Return and read the arrangement at whatever point you fall in an opening and are searching for an approach to get out.

3. Be careful with Reinforcement

Dynamic trading discharges adrenaline and endorphins. These synthetics can create sentiments of happiness, notwithstanding when you are losing cash. Thus, this urges addictive characters to take terrible positions, just to get the hurry.

4. Try not to Cut Corners

Your opposition burns through many hours of consummating methodologies, and you are in for a severe shock in the event that you hope to toss a couple of darts and leave with a benefit. It's far more terrible in the event that you cut corners in a mind-blowing remainder since that unfortunate propensity is a lot harder to break.

5. Grasp Simplicity

Concentrate on value activity, understanding that everything else is optional. Feel free to assemble complex, specialized markers, yet remember their essential capacity is to affirm or disprove what your prepared eye as of now observes.

6. Evade the Obvious

Benefit infrequently pursues the greater part. When you see an ideal exchange arrangement, almost certainly, every other person sees it too, planting you in the group and setting you up for disappointment.

7. Arrange Your Personal Life

Whatever is not right in your life will, in the end, persist into your trading execution. This is particularly risky on the off chance that you haven't profited, riches and the attractive extremity of plenitude and shortage.

8. Try not to Break Your Rules

You make trading principles to get you out of inconvenience when positions go seriously. On the off chance that you don't enable them to carry out their responsibility, you have lost your order and opened the entryway to significantly more noteworthy misfortunes.

9. Tune in to Your Intuition

Trading utilizes the scientific and imaginative sides of your cerebrum, so you have to develop both to prevail over the long haul. When you are alright with math, you can upgrade results with reflection, a couple of yoga stances, or a tranquil stroll in the recreation center.

10. Make Peace with Losses

Trading is one of only a handful couple of callings where losing cash each day is a characteristic way to progress. Each trading misfortune accompanies a significant market exercise in case you are available to the message.

11. Try not to Believe in a Company

In case you are excessively enamored with your trading vehicle, you offer an approach to defective basic leadership. You must gain by wastefulness, profiting while every other person is inclining the incorrect way.

12. Lose the Crowd

Long haul productivity requires situating in front of or behind the group, yet never in the group since that is the place savage techniques target. Avoid stock sheets and visit rooms. This is not kidding business, and everybody in those spots has an ulterior thought process.

13. Try not to Try to Get Even

Drawdowns are a characteristic piece of the merchant's life cycle. Acknowledge them effortlessly and adhere to the reliable methodologies you realize will, in the long run, recover your presentation on track.

14. Try not to Count Your Chickens

Like an exchange that is going your direction, yet the cash is not yours until you closeout. Lock in what you can as ahead of schedule as possible, with trailing stops or fractional benefits, so concealed hands cannot pickpocket your prosperity ultimately.

15. Watch for Early Warnings

Huge misfortunes once in a while happen without various specialized admonitions. Dealers routinely overlook those signs and would like to supplant keen control, setting themselves up for torment.

16. Pursue Your Discipline

Order cannot be instructed in a workshop or found in costly trading programming. Dealers burn through a great many dollars attempting to make up for their absence of poise, yet few understand that a long look in the mirror achieves a similar assignment at a lot less expensive cost!

17. Apparatuses Don't Think

Dealers compensate for deficient aptitudes with costly programming, prepackaged with a wide range of exclusive purchase and sell signals. These apparatuses meddle with important experience since you think the product is more brilliant than you are.

18. Play with Your Head

It's normal for dealers to copy their monetary saints, but at the same time, it's an ideal method to lose cash. Take in what you can from others at that point, back off, and set up your very own market personality; in light of your one-of-a-kind abilities and risk resistance.

19. Jettison the Paycheck Mentality

We're educated to pound through the stir week and afterward get our checks. This compensation for-exertion remunerate mindset clashes with the common progression of trading wins and misfortunes over the span of a year. Truth be told, insights show that most yearly benefits are set up for only a bunch of days the market is open for business.

20. Stay away from Market Gurus

It's your cash in question, not theirs. Remember that they're likely talking up their positions, trusting the energized prattle will expand their benefits, not yours.

Most by far of dealers neglect to tap their maximum capacity, in the end, trading in for cold hard currency their chips and discovering progressively customary approaches to profit. Become a pleased individual from the expert minority by following exemplary principles intended to keep a well-honed spotlight on productivity.

Chapter 11. Mistakes to Avoid in Options Trading

Trading options are more involved than trading stocks, so there are ample opportunities to make mistakes. It's important to take the approach of going small and slow at first so that you don't lose the shirt off your back. That said, if you run into mistakes, don't get too down about it. Dust yourself off and get up to fight another day. With that said, let's have a look at some common mistakes and how to avoid them.

Putting All Your Eggs in One Basket

While there is a difference between investing and trading, traders can learn a few things from our investor brothers (and most people are a little of both anyway). Don't let everything ride on one trade. If you take all the money you have and invest it in buying options for one stock, you're making a big mistake. Doing that is very risky, and as a beginning trader, you're going to want to mitigate your risk as much as possible. Betting on one stock may pay off sometimes, but more times than not, it's going to lead you into bankruptcy territory.

Investing More Than You Can

It's easy to get excited about options trading. The chances to make fast money and the requirements that you analyze the markets can be very enticing. Oftentimes that leads people into getting more excited than they should. A good rule to follow with investing is to make sure that you're setting aside enough money to cover living expenses every month, with a security fund for emergencies. Don't bet the farm on some sure thing by convincing yourself that you'll be able to make back twice as much money and so cover your expenses. Things don't always work out.

Going All in Before You're Ready

Another mistake is failing to take the time to learn options trading in real-time. Just like getting overly excited can cause people to bet too much money or put all their money on one stock, some people are impatient and don't want to take the time to learn the options markets by selling covered calls. It's best to start with covered calls and then move slowly to small deals buying call options. Leave put options until you've gained some experience.

Failure to Study the Markets

Remember, you need to be truly educated to make good options trades. That means you'll need to know a lot about the companies that you're either trying to profit from or that you're shorting. Options trading isn't possible without some level of guesswork, but make your guesses, educated guesses, and don't rely too much on hunches.

Not Getting Enough Time Value

Oftentimes, whether you're trading puts or calls, the time value is important. A stock may need an adequate window of time in order to beat the stock price, whether it's going above it or plunging below it. When you're starting out and don't know the markets as well as a seasoned trader, you should stick to options you can buy that have a longer time period before expiring.

Not Having Adequate Liquidity

Sometimes beginning investors overestimate their ability to play the options markets. Remember that if you buy an option, to make it work for you—you're going to need money on hand to buy stocks when the iron is hot. And you're going to need to buy 100 shares for every option contract. Before entering into the contract, make sure that you're going to be able to exercise your option.

Not Having a Grip on Volatility

If you don't understand volatility and its relation to premium pricing, you may end up making bad trades.

Failing to Have a Plan

Trading seems exciting, and when you're trading, you may lose the investors' mentality. However, traders need to have a strategic plan as much as investors do. Before trading, make sure that you have everything in place, including knowing what your goals are for the trades, having pre-planned exit strategies, developing criteria for getting into a trade so that you're not doing it on a whim or based on emotion.

Ignoring Expiration Dates

It sounds crazy, but many beginners don't keep track of the expiration date. Would you hate to see a stock go up in price and then hope it keeps going up, and it does, only to find out that your expiration date passed before you exercised your option?

Overleveraging

It's easy to spend huge amounts of money in small increments. This is true when it comes to trading options. Since stocks are more expensive, it's possible to get seduced by purchasing low-priced options. After all, options are available at a fraction of the cost that is required to buy stocks. And you might keep on purchasing them until you're overleveraged.

Buying Cheap Options

In many cases, buying cheap things isn't a good strategy. If you're buying a used car, while you might occasionally find a great car that is a good buy, in most cases, a car is cheap for a reason. The same applies to options trading. When it comes to options, a cheap premium probably denotes the option is out of the money. Sure, you save some money on a cheap premium, but when the expiration date comes, you might see the real reason the option contract was a cheap buy. Of course, as we described earlier, there may be cases where cheaper options have the capacity to rebound and become profitable by the time the expiry date arrives. But taking chances like that is best left to experienced traders.

Giving in to Panic

Remember that you have the right to buy or sell a stock if you've purchased an option. Some beginners panic and exercise their right far too early. This can happen because of fears that they'll be missing out on an opportunity with a call option or because of fears that a stock won't keep going down on a put.

Not Knowing How Much Cash You Can Afford to Lose

Going into options trading blindly is not a smart move. With each option trade you make, you need to have a clear idea of how much cash you have on hand to cover losses and exercising your options. You'll also want to know how much cash you can afford to lose if things go south.

Jumping Into Puts Without Enough Experience and Cash to Cover Losses

Remember, if you're selling puts, you will have to buy the stock at the strike price if the buyer exercises their option. This is a huge risk. The stock could have plunged in value, and you're going to have to buy the stock at the strike price, possibly leaving you with huge losses. Don't go into selling puts with your eyes closed; in fact, beginners are better off avoiding selling puts. But if you must do it, make sure you can absorb the losses when you bet wrong.

Piling It On

Most beginner mistakes are related to panic. If you're looking at losses on options, some beginners double and triple up, hoping to make it up when things turn better. Instead, they end up losing more money. Instead of giving in to panic, learn when to cut your losses and re-evaluate your trading strategy.

Staying in a Written Contract When You Should Get Out

If you've sold an option and it's looking like you might face a loss, you can always get out of it by selling.

Chapter 12. When to Enter and Exit the Trade

When you were a kid, did you ever play double Dutch jump rope? Double Dutch is where two people are swinging two lines, and a third person has to jump in for a bit before jumping out. As a kid, it was brutal and painful to find the right timing to jump in without getting hit with a rope. Entering into a trade can be just as nerve-wracking. You can be set up to join the business and stress yourself with questions like, "Do I jump in now? How about now?" But with some strategic planning and practice, you can find the best area you would like to jump in regularly.

The entry point in a trade is the point at which you want to buy an asset. It's the starting bid in your business. Whether you are trading stocks or options, you will always have to have an entry point. Having a good plan for when you will enter into a trade is beneficial because it means that you won't have to drive yourself mad. It also means that you won't be making an emotional choice regarding when to enter.

Choosing a good entry point means analyzing the chart for support, resistance, and trend. Look at the past movement of the table and find the support and resistance. Then, look at the direction. Has the chart been moving in a specific trend line? Or has it been in a stage of consolidation? Or a period where the market has remained relatively steady? With a stock that has a trend line, you can choose a point right after a rebound. For example, let's say stock ABC was trading at $60 in November before dropping to $58. As the number starts to rise again, you can see if the chart seems like it's going to return to trend. If yes, then you can place your entry point at $60 and wait to see if the trend will continue upward.

In the case of a stock that is at a stage \of the neutral movement, then your support and resistance lines will be horizontal, and the chart will remain between those two lines. In this case, follow the pattern of the movement and again place your entry point at the price where a rebound is likely to happen. This should be close to the support line. There's a good chance that the stock value will rise again towards the resistance in this case.

Let's put this into action.

Chose two different practice charts. One should have a stock that is trending upwards, and one should have stock that is steady and isn't trending in a particular direction. Taking the one that is trending upward, draw the trend line in the support line position. From there, choose a location that offers you a small swing up. At what point would you enter the swing? At what price point? How long would you remain in the swing? Do the same for the chart that is remaining steady. What location above the support line would you enter into the trade? It's easy to do this with past maps because everything is already lined up. But take the time to analyze the chart. What makes specific swings more successful, and what makes them unsuccessful?

Now try with a future practice trade. Again, find a chart from a stock that you would be interested in purchasing. Map out your lines, find the zone you'll trade-in, and then choose an entry point either in the present or the future. After that, watch the stock for several days. Would your trade have panned out? If yes, why? And if no, why not? All of this practice allows you to try out deals before investing any capital into them. Once you feel a bit more confident about entry points, move on to learn about exit points.

When you enter into the trade, you need to make sure that your risk/reward ratio makes the deal worth it. Once you calculate the rate, you can determine at what point you can exit the trade to make the reward worth it.

Now we're going to learn how to exit a trade. It is essential to have an exit strategy. Without an exit strategy, you will choose to leave a business whenever you feel like it, which can cause you some losses. You may exit too early or too late. It is better to have a strategy in place so that you know exactly when you'll exit. For example, if you determine that you would like to make a specific amount of profit, that's your exit point. Don't go past that.

As you throw it, momentum keeps it going higher but at a slower pace until it reaches its peak. At this point, energy is zero, and the ball falls back into your hands. In a swing trade, you want to exit the deal before the momentum reaches zero., not at the peak, but before the summit. This is because most traders will be looking to sell at the height of the trade, which will cause a drop in the market—selling early before the estimated peak is a risk. It might mean that you lose out if the ball continues to go much higher than you anticipated. However, you will still have made it again before any reversal happens, and you can always buy back into the trend if you want to.

When looking at the charts for a stock, you should keep in mind your entry position and where you would like to exit. If the stock has stayed steady over the last bit of time and remains in its range, then looking at the support and resistance can give you a good idea of where to exit. If you entered near the support, then you can determine at what point you would like to exit. This depends on a lot of factors like your tolerance for risk and how long you want to stay in the trade. Generally speaking, if the stock value keeps increasing, you want to exit before it hits the resistance. Remember, in swing trading, it's all about small gains, not large ones, so it's better to leave with some profit rather than no profit.

With your support and resistance marked on a chart, you can also look for key indicators that show you that it's time to sell. One of these indicators is either if the stock value exceeds its resistance or if it drops below its support numbers. This can mean that it's starting to trend in one specific direction, but it could also mean that these little breakouts will backtrack into what it was sitting at before. If the stock value exceeds its resistance and you haven't sold yet, then you can choose to wait until it returns to its range or see if it will be the start of a new trend. This decision, again, depends on how much risk you're willing to take.

There are a couple of things you can do to make sure that you are not staying in a trade too long. The first one is to set a stop-loss. A stop-loss is a tool that will sell your shares if the stock price goes too low. The other option is to place a limited order. A limit order will sell your trades once they've reached your set peak value. Let's say that the current stock price for ABC is $20 per share when you enter. You can choose to place your limit order at $25 a share. You can also set it at a certain percentage point for profit. This means that at the $25 mark, your broker will sell your shares. This can be good because it can limit your losses, but it can also prevent you from taking advantage of a possible trend. So once again, make a decision based on your tolerance for risk.

As you make your exit strategy, you should ask yourself a few questions. You should know how long you are willing to stay in a trade, how much risk you can tolerate, and at what point you want to get out. These three things will help you make a good exit strategy. For example, when asking yourself how long you want to stay in a trade, you can think about how long you want your capital to be tied up, what indicators you're looking for that will cause you to sell, etc.

When considering how much risk you're willing to take, try a few different scenarios. Also, think about what a profit is to you. Is it $1 per share a decent profit, or do you want to make more? Finally, consider when you want to leave the trade. You should have this written down clearly. Are you going to leave the business once you've made a guaranteed profit, once you hit the resistance level, or once you see another indication that it's time to go? When you've made your plan, you must stick to it. This will help you remain emotionally objective when trading.

Once you've made your exit plan, it's time again to practice. Look at some past charts and analyze where you would have entered and exited the trade, based on the indicators like support and resistance or based on the moving average. Analyze every piece of a move. Why would a specific exit point have worked or failed? Afterward, try this again with a future chart. You can either do this in a simulation or using your chart website of choice. Pick a stock you want to follow and find an entry point you think will work for you. Then, using your exit strategy, determine when you will exit the chart. Spend a few days looking at your plan as the table moves forward. Did your plan work? Are there other ways you could have executed it? Keep practicing, don't just do this with one chart, and think you're ready to start trading.

Conclusion

Options provide elective procedures for investors to benefit from protection trading. There's an assortment of methodologies, including various combinations of options, hidden assets, and different derivatives. Fundamental techniques for novices incorporate buying calls, buying puts, selling covered calls, and buying protective puts. There are preferences to trading options instead of fundamental assets, such as drawback assurance and leveraged returns; however, there are also inconveniences like the prerequisite for forthright premium installment.

Everyone should try paper exchange options if, despite everything, you haven't discovered your trading style or technique or if you're hoping to explore new trading systems and ideas. Paper trading is also an extraordinary tool for developing your certainty.

Trading is very difficult when you have money on hold, and feeling begins to sneak in, so working out your certainty can have a major impact.

Your objective as a broker ought to be to make progress from paper trading to live trading as smooth as could be allowed. Jumping into the intricate universe of options without legitimate learning about this instrument can prompt genuine losing exchanges. In case you're one of the cynics of paper trading, we urge you to try it out and test new methodologies before going with them on your live account.

The options may seem irresistible, but it's easy to understand if you know some key points. Investor portfolios generally consist of several asset classes. These can be stocks, bonds, ETFs, and even investment funds. Options are a second class of assets and, when used properly, offer many benefits that equity and ETFs cannot.

With all this insight into the options market, you should be able to carry out a trade from start to finish successfully. You must, however, note that the options business is not for every investor. It can get sophisticated and dangerous if you do not put the information outlined in this manuscript into practice.

It is now clear to you whether this is an investment that you want to try out or not. If you're into it, then you're going to have to decide the kind of trader you want to be. You can either be a day trader, a long-term trader, or a short-term trader. As a day trader, you're going to have the advantage of making a few trades that close quickly.

This option is perfect for you if you're interested in making small profits. Otherwise, consider long-term trading that can span over 30 days but with incredible profits.

Trading on options also involves choosing the underlying security that you would wish to connect your options too. This may be in the form of commodities, stock, or foreign currency. Each currency has its characteristics, and the liquidity status also matters. Commodities are good but very volatile, currencies trade most of the time, but economic news items easily influence the prices. Stocks experience a rapid change in prices overnight.

To earn a steady income as a trader in options, you have to set your goals. How much do you plan on earning each week? What is your trading capital? Which stocks in the marketing are you looking to target or focus on? How many hours do you want to dedicate to the trade? Consider getting a mentor or joining a group where you can learn and ask questions to help you stay on course.

If you are already doing some job, you can consider investing at least an hour every day in the trade. Study the market and begin to analyze what is going on in the options trading market. Commit yourself to study, reading, attending seminars, and learning about the options trading market, always ensuring that you are growing in your knowledge of the field to succeed in the market. Learn new methods and strategies for maximizing profitability.

Look for a good broker that matches your goals and start with a basic plan. A good broker will provide you with the tools, resources, and support to succeed in the market. There are lots of brokers out there with great tools to make you succeed. Get a recommendation. Check their fees and prices before making a final decision.

Always make sure you use the corresponding strategy that matches the analysis you have made via the market. There are a lot of basic and advanced strategies that you can use to excel. Use the simple and easy-to-understand ones.

Using technical analysis to analyze stock trends and volatility in the stock market, but always endeavor to follow and read the fundamental events surrounding the underlying stock you are looking to trade-in. Practice or try to combine both technical and fundamental analysis in making trading decisions.

Necessarily, options trading methodologies are exceedingly intended to support specialists, experienced financial specialists, and traders just as the tenderfoots, and even the individuals who are keen on seeking after this art. These systems for options trading are delegated a few devices to enable you to begin and keep up such the extreme status of your speculation. Options preparing might be given to any individual who has the energy, intrigue, and excitement over this endeavor.